The Fisherman

El Rose

BARNARD
PUBLISHING LTD.

The Fisherman © El Rose

Cover design by Rein Lee

ISBN 978-1-7395845-6-6

Barnard Publishing

Mold, Wales

barnard.publishing@gmail.com

www.barnardpublishing.co.uk

The Fisherman

For the Neurodiverse, may you love yourselves.
For the others, may you learn.

INTRODUCTION

I started writing this collection to fulfil weekly prompts in an Experimental Writing module in my Undergraduate degree, they would eventually become a short portfolio which I submitted as my final module project. It was written, at the time, by an author who wanted to have something to get feedback from and for whom poetry is less about the politics of taking a stand or making a statement, and much more to do with processing her own experiences, her own feelings and memories. She wrote the poems fast, as she writes all things, and she handed them in with little editing but a whole lot of heartfelt defence in her commentary. Looking back at it now, I still love the snippets of vulnerability I put into the project.

I write that 'each piece is a different method of communication'. I write 'it is not intended to be professional'. I write 'our discussion of the moon as the link to the fisherman illustrates how what would likely be an irrelevant aspect of the experience to those processing the memory through neurotypical minds was, to us, just as important as the primary subject'.

These are the fundamental tenets of this collection. It is not meant to be professional; I scribble out words and make mistakes and trace over my own handwriting because I have known since I started to write in cursive that my use of the pen is typically illegibly. Each piece continues to be a different method of communication; from letters, to games, to a whole accompanying digital space made by a dear friend, Ada, who worked alongside me as this project grew and grew and grew. And, most importantly to me, this collection continues to prioritise the seemingly 'irrelevant' and the dismissal of neurotypical conventions, expectations, or understandings.

These are poems to baffle. To confuse. They are poems to question the definition of poetry. They are an activity book to write in your own words. They are mine, now, and as you read this, they become yours. Make what sense you want out of them. Tell me about them. Or don't.

My understanding of them is based in my experiences of being a white, queer, autistic, anxious, brown-haired, 5'6", cisgender, academic, stubborn, asexual, sapphic, cat-loving, dog-hating, English speaking, British, BSL-learning, plushie-collecting, hayfever-having, eldest sister, determined, sappy, woman. You won't be the same as me. I won't be the same as you. We are different. We are diverse. I cannot fully understand you, you cannot fully understand me. But I can stand shoulder to shoulder with you. I can help you see and help you feel seen. That's what I'm trying to do now. I'm not on a weekly deadline for a module class anymore. I'm just here, choosing which words to share with you, for you.

THE SIGHT

Fisherman

He
Watches
Us
Watching
Him turns
Back to fish
And dinner and
Solitude
In the
Dark of
This late
Night
B r I g ht
Warm
Heat Fire
In the dark
Line pole in the sand on its
own no he
Independent
Focus

Sea

Sprayspray
Crashing white horses
Foam
Blue turned navy
Rocks I climbed not s o long
ago
Ro ll ing hitting s a n d to
wards
us c o m I n g c l o s e r
I drank
Half the
O c e a n
Today
W h o k n o w s
W h e re a n d yet
Whitefoam its catching up
but
Bu
But it
All
This
Now

Cliff

READ THIS
LIKE SAND
IN YOUR SHO
ES LIKE ME
MORIES IN
YOUR DREAM
S FONTS TH
AT REMIN
D YOU OF Y
OUR CHILD
HOOD PU
BLISHER
POSTER
DID HE
MAKE P
OSTERS ON
STRANGER
DANGER? DO
ES HE HAVE A
HOUSE OR

JUST THAT
CAMPER O
N THE ROA
D? HE IS
ALL I DON'T
KNOW I
N THE MO
ONLIGH
T DID
HE LOS
E LOVE
S IN ONE
PLAGUE
ALREAD
Y? EAT
WELL
SIR

Grass

sheercliffuphereandwedidnotc
limbherebutI
must
thinkitssimilartobeforeanditst
retchedsofarh
owfarIknowbutdoIknow?

Rocks

Rockrockrock
Rockbehinghim
Therocksbehindhim
Himasilhouetteashadow
Thecentreandnothing
All at once
Rockrockrock
Barnacles grip
Seaweed slip
And
Rockrock
Rock we climbed rock
Rock here this morning
Rockrockrock

Steps

A RAMP BEHIND
AWAY
To
Stairs I
Sit on the
Next morning

Stars

s t a r s
t r s
a r s t a
s t s st
r s a
s t a r s

DEFINE YOUR TERMS

A creature who
wades in water
and on mud-slick
banks of bodies
of blue in
order to
catch fish
or other
aquatic animals

An item of
identity latched
onto the
skeleton of
personhood

FISHERMAN (Noun) → Plural! Fishermen

A career prospect

a role
a person
fulfils

False alarms
silent to you
and managed
by her
strength
of will

Omnipresent
outside this
space

FEAR
(Noun + Verb) → Causes:

A feeling of
impending
pain or sorrow

A man in
the shadows

Headlights
swinging
screams
biting

Tongue of the ocean

The foundation of a castle

Critters of frozen gazes

Hitchhikers of socks

SAND (NOUN)

The start of a plant

Bane of sandwiches

Found; underfoot

Divine to wood and smokers' lungs alike

Pickpocket of chills

FIRE (NOUN)

Vanquisher of darkness

And: A killer

Heavy
and
empty

A friend

An absence
of physical
light

DARKNESS → origins:
(NOUN)

A loss
of visual
spatial
awareness

safe
and
ultimately
murderous

Everlasting
and
untouchable

The start
of it all
and of
nothing

Trying without
end to push and
push and push
and push
for
CONTINUING your
(verb)   understanding

Pushing
onward
despite
mistakes

Question:
Do you see it
yet?

Reaching
heights of
speckled shins and
unshaved thighs   The ticking
                         noise of the
                         countdown
              T I D E → Hitting lows
              (NOUN)   of fantasy
The   worlds and
lapping love   pressure, pressure,
of a clock   How long are /pressure,/
hand falling we staying;
down and round
                         Until the sea
                         nicks us out

              The fishing   his rod
the slippage line
of sea and   and   Him
      sand   the curve
the sun   of the   the give
                 note
          Her TRIANGLE   Him
The shape ←   (NOUN) →
She couldnt   the
shake   the ocean moon   her
                              The
      the
      land   the   point: Three
            bridge of
            braided plastic

17

Ptolemy's
one of
gourty-eight ⌐

Five ←
stars

⌐ CASSIOPEIA
    (Noun)

↓
A rough
'w' in
shape

She cried under
her once, head
tipped back,
↑ kitchen light
                bathing
                her
                goosebumps,
                losing
                grasp of
↓   gravity
Describe!   as
                the
Beloved   sky
beauty   spun
                round her
                and her

FISHERMAN
[Noun]
A role a person fulfils. An item of identity latched onto the skeleton of personhood. A career prospect. A creature who wades in water and on mud-slick banks of bodies of blue in order to catch fish or other aquatic animals.

Plural: Fishermen

FEAR
[Noun & Verb]
Omnipresent outside this space. A feeling of impending pain or sorrow. False alarms silent to you and managed by her strength of will.

Causes: A Man In The Shadows
Headlights Swinging
Screams Biting

SAND
[Noun]
The start of a pearl. The foundation of a castle. Tongue of the ocean. Bane of sandwiches. Hitchhikers of socks. Gritters of frozen faces.

Found: Underfoot

FIRE
[Noun]
Vanquisher of darkness. Pickpocket of chills. Divine to wood and smokers' lungs alike.

And: A Killer.

DARKNESS
[Noun]
An absence of physical light. A loss of visual spatial awareness. A friend. Everlasting and untouchable. Heavy and empty. Safe and ultimately murderous.

Origins: The Start Of It All And Of Nothing

CONTINUING
[Verb]
Pushing onward despite mistakes. Trying without end to push and push and push and push for your understanding.
Question: Do You See It Yet?

TIDE
[Noun]
The ticking noise of the countdown. The lapping love of a clock hand falling down and round. Reaching heights of freckled shins and unshaved thighs. Hitting lows of fantasy worlds and pressure, pressure, pressure.
How Long Are We Staying: Until The Sea Kicks Us Out

CASSIOPEIA
[Noun]
Five stars. Ptolemy's one of fourty-eight. She cried under her once, head tipped back, kitchen light bathing her goosebumps, losing grasp of gravity as the sky spun round her and her. A rough 'w' in shape.
Describe: Beloved Beauty

TRIANGLE
[Noun]
The shape she couldn't shake. Him, his rod, the fire. The fishing line, the slippage of sea and sand, and the curve of the pole. Her, the moon, the sun. Him, the moon, her. The ocean, the land, the bridge of braided plastic.
The Point: Three

Consider the alternatives: The colour green
The sharp lights of phone screens
The opaque density of night
The surety of the way
The crunch of shells
The stick of toasted sugar
The bite-back of jokes to be misunderstood
The sharing of coats and scarves
The freedom of distance

Consider the building blocks: The colour blue
The distant lights
Reaching your homes
The knowledge of what a
Shadow means
The ability of question
So much of nothing
The wet of water
The tick of the heart
The warmth of people
The community of a group
The weight of your note

CONSIDER

Consider the rhythm

The song of somewhere new
            The fishing pole that
                        curves
The promise of a later shower to be
clean
        The answers to near-enough
                    everything
The net of being an eldest daughter
The tips of the
    moon's reach
                The fire-caught flash
            of a dimple
            The possibility of his sea-salt
                        soup
The reflected depth of
                    your soul

Consider

The electric captures
of your forgotten swimwear the
The van on the splinters
standing the next roadside
unbothered morning of root the
the near
of the transient table
The cycle of the tide
The sand in your sheets finalities
The names lost to pine two-fold
days later not a field
The reunion in a
at home

The satisfaction through
of plans
followed

Consider the building blocks:

The colour blue
The death lights reaching
your nerves
The knowledge of what a
moving shadow means
The ability to question much
of nothing
The wet of water
The tick of the beach
The warmth of people
The community of a group
The weight of your role

Consider the rhymes:

The song of somewhere new
The fishing pole that curves
The promise of a later shower
to be clean
The answers to near-enough
everything
The net of being an eldest
daughter
The tip of the moon's reach
The fire-caught flash of a
dimple
The possibility of his sea-salt
soup
The reflected depth of your
soul

Consider the alternatives:

The colour green
The sharp lights of phone
screens
The opaque density of night
The surety of the way
The crunch of shells
The stick of toasted sugar
The bite-back of jokes to be
misunderstood
The sharing of coats and
scarves
The freedom of distance

Consider the finalities:

The electric captures of your
swimwear
The forgotten splinters of soot
The van on the road the next
morning standing unbothered
The peace of the transience
The cycle of the tide
The sand in your sheets
The names lost to time not
two days later
The reunion in a field at
home
The satisfaction of plans
followed through

Read stood there
    think   frozen but he
      he checked the   moved
           line

he stoked the fire and hung a
pot, cast iron darkness beside
his silhouette
He turned to watch us walk by
a motley group of students
    Mostly straight.
       Mostly couples.

   Loud and immature on their
beach bonfire trip.
No one had a screwdriver so
I turned the screws into the
nuts with my fingertips.
     proud of my achievement
in the dark. Leadership material.
  The little dipper. Cassiopeia.
space cowboys and casting spells
costs blood. Irish sea waves
lapping at his shore. There were

no fish when I swam earlier.
Only rocks grazing my ~~knees~~
girlish knees and seaweed
tangling in my fingertips. Maybe
the fish have come for him.
Following the golden moonlight.

Read stood there
          think frozen but he moved
               he checked the line
he stoked the fire and hung a
pot, cast iron darkness beside
his silhouette
He turned to watch us walk by
a motley group of students
          Mostly straight.
                    Mostly couples.
          Loud and immature on their
          beach bonfire trip.
No one had a screwdriver so
I turned the screws into the
Nuts with my fingertips.
          Proud of my achievement
in the dark. Leadership material.
          The little dipper. Cassiopeia.
Space cowboys and casting spells
costs blood. Irish sea waves
lapping at his shore. There were
no fish when I swam earlier.

Only rocks grazing my knees
girlish knees and seaweed
tangling in my fingertips. Maybe
the fish have come for him.
Following the golden moonlight.

I like when it's a crescent

moon ↗

I like seeing the shadow of
the moon and knowing
its there even as I mostly
see the shiny crescent
and isn't it awesome
to think
about the
silence of that
too?

aint it cool,
really freaking cool
that we see the same
moon?

to think hey

the sun is
over
there

I looked at it tonight
and thought.
wow its so bright and
beautiful — and its the
same moon
that's the same
moon as your moon

in that
direction
we are
a triangle
me, the moon
and the sun

me / looking at the
moon while at the
sun, turned
away from us
me and you
me observe
the moon
observing
the sun

hehe
you're
such an
English
student

we'll get you
to play outer
wilds next

30

I saw this like two
minutes ago

she had such long
fur but shinely
clearly still only
a baby

didn't
have
anything
to say
about

Serendipity

that
found
gift x

soul time

trains are so
cool

love trains ♡

hate people
on them

i always want
to send you these for
some reason

you are a paradox of tactile — and also
you love language and scared of touch it's
great

where did you go ? — did not reply

I love this
i have this

the tension

suspense
the

proun

parcel?
letter or a
Fri this is a
suspense
dates mixed up

lmao the suspense

okay you surprise
25ᵗʰ earliest I get there I'd
hope you cheese get there I got my

imagine
i'm parallel
playing in
your room
idk

31

tragedy is so good

if I did a masters I'd do it on tragedy and how its handled with queer characters/romances vs straight

the hadestown line "it's a sad song, but we sing it anyway" always gets me

!!!! 'its written and cannot be undone' 'the reader knows it will be a tragedy and still the hope in a situation that shouldn't have hope! ♡

I don't want to be incapable — I feel so much love from you of love — from every interaction. you love everything

— the one theatre thing I want to see actually no— there's two, it's that and no exit.

Literature at english og degree level under the hugepiles the gay girl thing I can hardly see but hey good job. I'm crying, perhaps

did you sign up to daily dracula

I did / I did

you! / yeah i'm —?

catching up on the first few days now

MOON

I like when it's a crescent

I like seeing the shadow of
the moon and knowing it's
there even as I mostly see the
shiny crescent and isn't it
awesome to think about the
science of that too?
to think hey
the sun is over there
in that direction
we are a triangle. me, the
moon and the sun
me and you looking at the
moon who's looking at the
sun, turned away from us for
tonight
we observe the moon
observing the sun

Ain't it cool, really freaking
cool that we see the same
moon?

we'll get you to play Outer
Wilds next

I looked at it tonight and
thought wow it's so bright
and beautiful
and it's the same moon that's
the same moon as your moon

MOON

:0

love trains <3
hate the people on them <3

that bowl gets it

33

I love this

I'm dying

hehe you're such an English
student

Trains are so cool

SOUP MUG

I always want to send you
these for some reason

you are a paradox of tactile
love language and also
scared of touch it's great

but hey good job

I can hardly see the gay
flirting under the huge piles of
degree level English literature

I don't want to be incapable
of love

I feel so much love from you
from every interaction you
love everything

serendipity
she had such long fur but
skinny clearly still only a
baby

I saw this like two minutes
ago

I did I did
you!
?

Where did you go : (
?
did you sign up to daily   did not reply : (: (: (: (: (
Dracula

yeah I'm catching up on the
first few days now

Imagine I'm parallel playing in
your room idk

35

works for me

didn't have anything to say

ah okay

okay your surprise doesn't
get there 'til 25th earliest I
got my dates mixed up

<3

a parcel

lmao the suspense

the tension

if I did a masters I'd do it on
tragedy and how it's handled
with queer characters/
romances vs straight

fr is this a letter or a parcel?

the suspense

tragedy is so good

the hadestown line "it's a sad
song but we sing it anyway"
always gets me

the one theatre thing I want to
see

actually no there's two it's that
and 'no exit'

!!! 'it's written and cannot be undone' 'the reader knows it will be a tragedy and still hopes otherwise', the hope in a situation that shouldn't have hope!

<3

DEAR SIR

Dear Sir,

I call you 'sir' out of polite ingrained manners and the traditional criteria of a handwritten letter. I'm not sure that you are a 'sir'. You were on the beach late in the dark evening, moon rising, with a fishing rod and a fire under a cooking pot. It wasn't warm enough for a late night supper on the beach even if there /were/ fish or crabs in that cove's water-logged lungs. Surely you knew it was hopeless?

I considered, at the time, if calling you 'sir' was to assume too much. Presumptions of gender expression, of our British rules of class, of the nature of your behaviour. Part of me asks forgiveness for continuing to assume the worst of you. Branding you a vagabond, a drunkard, cast out and dirty and prone to harming women in

the shadows. Part of me, louder,
defensive in its ~~vigorous~~ reasonings,
argues that it is a case of safety.
If I do not assume the worst,
I will be hurt. Taken apart.
killed, one way or the other. Assume
the worst and stay alive. ~~suspect~~
Suspicion is safety.

But can't I suspect with more
human respect for you? I wonder
if you would understand my
thoughts. Would you debate, as I
am debating myself then and
now, with me on points like

'I could be evil without
   being dirty'

'seeming homeless does not
mean I could punch you for
looking at me wrong, whether I
have a home or not, by choice or
not'.   Would you challenge my logic?
I am, I would encourage you to join in.

I hold onto the darkness and the male presentation of your body, your movements, your sheer confidence in being out alone at night, as my excuse for thinking ill of you. I was scared of you then. I feel the leftover imprint of that anxiety even now. It's nuanced, you know? There's no right way or wrong. No correct reaction or wrong one. I had my reasons, I had my prejudices.

I'm sorry.
And I am also not,
Yours,

40

Dear sir,

I call you 'sir' out of polite ingrained manners and the traditional criteria of a handwritten letter. I'm not sure that you are a 'sir'. You were on the beach late in the dark evening, moon rising, with a fishing rod and a fire under a cooking pot. It wasn't warm enough for a late night supper on the beach even if there were fish or crabs in that cove's water-logged lungs. Surely you knew it was hopeless?

I considered, at the time, if calling you 'sir' was to assume too much. Presumptions of gender expression, of our British rules of class, of the nature of your behaviour. Part of me asks forgiveness or continuing to assume the worst of you. Branding you a vagabond, a drunkard, cast out and dirty and prone to harming women in the shadows. Part of me, louder, defensive in its vigorous reasoning, argues that it is a case of safety. If I do not assume the worst, I will be hurt. Taken apart. Killed, one way or the other. Assume the worst and stay alive. Suspect Suspicion is safety.

But can't I suspect with more human respect for you? I wonder if you would understand my thoughts. Would you debate, as I am debating myself then and now, with me on points like 'I could be evil without being dirty', 'seeming homeless does not mean I could punch you for looking at me wrong, whether I have a home or not, by choice or not'. Would you challenge my logic? I am, I would encourage you to join in.

I hold on to the darkness and the male presentation of your body, your movements, your sheer confidence in being out alone at night, as my excuse for thinking ill of you. I was scared of you then. I feel the leftover imprint of that anxiety even now. It's nuanced, you know? There's no right way or wrong. No correct reaction or wrong one. I had my reasons, I had my prejudices.

I'm sorry.

And I am also not.

Yours,
~ ~ ~

FLOWCHART TO GAMING

Do you go to the beach?

↓ Yes   ↓ No

↓   ↓

She needs you to lead   Then what do you miss?

↓ Why?   ↓ On my own?

↓   ↓

take her with you.
okay.

↓ Let her lead   ↓ Take point   ↗ gather everyone inside

↓ "no." okay.   ↓ gather everyone outside   ↓ Explain the plan

↗   ↓ Explain the plan →   ↓ Start leaving you and her ahead

↓

No one really listens but follow
nonetheless

The road is dark, no streetlights.
Do you remember the way?

Ask her for help

"I think this way"
okay.   → Right

                              have you
                              got the
                              pit?

Yes.
Yes, I know

They're walking
in the road

Left   yes   Call for
            It's   NO   them to
            not   shit.   stay to
            very   the side
            heavy

                                        walk
                              turn   backwards
                              back   There's ← to watch
                                     so many.   them

                    A car is coming

Shine your light
on these faces and
shout

Call and wave
them in,
stay safe

You sure
can be loud

working with kids does that to
a person

They pick up the call, your words
echo back

and back

and back

and
back

and
back

and
back

and
back

and
back

and
back

and
back ← and
back

and back

and back

and
back

and
back → Everyone is safe ←

and
back

↓

Do you have the supplies?

↓ NO

↓

Send people back

I'm trying not to listen

↓

why?

There's so many of them and we are not the same

↓

similar?

maybe.   barely.

↓   ↓

It's time to cross the road

↓

↓ YES

↓

what can you hear?

↓

what can't I hear?

↓

people like me.

watch the night.

stand guard

trust them

we've been here before → yes. ← take off your shoes?

we aren't

No.

but we are

alone.

less

point him out to her

they're turned back

they're lost to us

Is he safe?

Must we find them?

He is not paying undue attention to us

Or care for our less?

watch him

get people moving to leave him in peace

MEMORISE

HIM ← see him ← come back to him

Leave.

1. Do you go to the beach?
Yes [Go to 3]
No [Go to 2]

2. Then what do you miss?

3. She needs you to lead
Why? [Go to 4]
On my own? [Go to 4]

4. 'Take her with you.' Okay.
Let her lead [Go to 5]
Take point [Go to 6]

5. 'No.' Okay.
Take point [Go to 6]

6. You're taking point.
Gather everyone inside [Go to 8]
Gather everyone outside [Go to 7]

7. Everyone is outside.
Explain the Plan [Go to 8]
Start leaving [Go to 9]

8. You explain your Plan.
You leave [Go to 9]

9. Start leaving, you and her ahead.
No one really listens but follow nonetheless [Go to 10]

10. The road is dark, no streetlights. Do you remember the way?
Yes. Yes, I know [Go to 12]
Ask her for help [Go to 11]

11. 'I think this way.' Okay.
Right [Go to 13]
Left [Go to 17]

12. They're walking in the road.
Call for them to stay to the side [Go to 16]
Walk backwards to watch them [Go to 16]

13. Have you got the pit?
Yes [Go to 14]
No [Go to 15]

14. It's not very heavy.
Turn back [Go to 11, Choose B]

15. Shit.

16. There's so many.
[Go to 17]

17. A car is coming.
Shine your light on these faces and shout [Go to 18]
Call and wave them in, stay safe [Go to 18]

18. You sure can be loud.
[Go to 19]

19. Working with kids does that to a person.
[Go to 20]

20. They pick up the call, your words echo back.
And back [Go to 21]
And back [Go to 27]
And back [Go to 22]

21. And back.
And back [Go to 23]
And back [Go to 24]

22. And back.
And back [Go to 23]
And back [Go to 25]

23. And back.
And back [Go to 24]
And back [Go to 27]

24. And back.
And back [Go to 27]
And back [Go to 25]

25. And back.
And back [Go to 26]
And back [Go to 27]

26. And back.
And back [Go to 27]

27. Everyone is safe.
[Go to 28]

28. Do you have the supplies?
Yes [Go to 30]
No [Go to 29]

29. Send people back.

30. What can you hear?
What can't I hear? [Go to 31]
I'm trying not to listen [Go to 32]

31. People like me.

32. Why?
There's so many of them and we are not the same [Go to 33]

33. Similar?
Maybe [Go to 34]
Barely [Go to 34]

34. It's time to cross the road. Watch the night.
Stand guard [Go to 35]
Trust them [Go to 36]

35. We've been here before.
Yes [Go to 37]

36. Take off your shoes?
Yes [Go to 37]
No [Go to 37]

37. We aren't alone.
But we are less [Go to 38]
Point him out to her [Go to 40]

38. We are less.
They've turned back [Go to 39]
They're lost to us [Go to 39]
[Go to 40]

39. Must we find them? Or care for our less?

40. Is he safe?
He is not paying undue attention to us [Go to 41]
He is not paying undue attention to us [Go to 42]

41. Get people moving to leave him in peace.
Come back to him [Go to 43]

42. Watch him.
[Go to 44]

43. See him.
[Go to 44]

44. MEMORISE HIM.
[Leave.]

GALLERY HALL-INTERIOR - NO
INDICATION OF TIME

The hall is one large room. Off-white
blank walls, no windows. Shiny
luminate wood flooring, a birch colour,
darker than expected in the low light,
that clacks under heels and boots.

The lights come from ~~the corners~~
the corners of the room, nowhere
else.

They shine a ~~navy blue~~ deep navy
blue, bordering on the darkness
of the night sky, the ocean as you
gaze into the absence of life in
the midnight depths.

One ~~other~~ light flickers in the back
of the room, a red-orange,
suggestive of a flame.

The only sound in the room is the hushed breathing of a group of university students behind the camera as they enter the room out of frame.

A crackle, supposedly from the fire that cannot yet be seen because, hanging randomly from a dark ceiling, painted with silver dots to resemble stars not quite in true constellations, by thin strings of brown twine are hundreds of sheets of paper. All A4 size.

These papers are covered in what looks like black ink but is not in focus yet and so are unreadable; the intentions of the pages are, as such, invisible to the viewer.

There are so many that one cannot see entirely through the room to the other side.

The shadows of light from the fire are the only indiciations that there is something other than paper in the room.

The camera lingers, taking in the room, as if eyesight is adjusting to the darkness. It feels like a blanket, heavy and nearly physical.

Students start to ~~talk~~ move in front of the camera, spreading out to explore the pages.

~~Students~~ They are dressed in casual ~~~~ summer clothes: shawls, shorts, vest ~~tops~~, sunglasses pushed up into hair, thinner fabric hijabs to suit the summer heat, one person is in a one-piece swimsuit with a wrap skirt around their waist.

All that is heard is their ~~footsteps~~, soft but noticeable, and the hush of fabric moving, breaths had.

A beat.

The camera watches them enter this landscape of paper.

Then we follow after them, carving our own path.

We go past one piece of paper and focus in on the one behind.

It shows a swirl of writing, a circular path leading into the centre of the page where a crudely drawn silhouette stands in front of a triangle and a gently curving line.

We move past, weaving left and right.

No pages are touched, they are absolutely still throughout the entire room.

There are shadows of passing students in the corners of the eye, forging their own paths, lingering as they wish.

The next page we stop at is a letter, written on lined paper. It ends abruptly as if a page is missing. We do not stay long enough for the viewer to read it all.

We come to stand next to two students, a shared experience of the page. It is a conversation. Multiple conversations. One of the students leaves to the left.

A beat.

The other student leaves, turning back.

A beat. Another.

A crackle like a log falling on a fire. A glare of warm light bursts in the murky background

We move on.

We pass by two, three, four pages

We stop.

The orange-red-warm light is brighter now. The papers are thinner in number. A wall can be made out ahead. A light at the end of the tunnel.

The slivers of wall visible are painted semi-realistically as scenery. A vision of cliffs rising high, the night sky above in the darkest hours, a yellow moon glowing faintly, the ocean waves of a cove at the bottom.

The crackling of fire is constant background noise, it is not intrusive.

The paper we have stopped at is taking up most of the frame, there is the feeling that (something) is behind it. The paper shows this script.

A heat.

A rough cough, a man's, elderly.

The paper is pushed away by a hand revealing the final shot.

A small fire, a ring of seashore stones around it to keep it contained. A pitiful amount of sand underneath it and under the feet of an elderly man dressed in dark colours.

A fishing rod is stuck in the sand, left of the fire, curving the line further left flung to the empty corner of the room.

The man stands to the right of the fire, barely more than a silhouette.

An unkempt beard, bushy but not huge. A woolen beanie hat. A fisherman's waterproof trousers. Stocky worn work boots. Winter jacket.

He faces his fishing line, unmoving. Breathing gently, slowly.

We linger on him, not zooming in, not changing focus.

Students start to assemble in line with the camera.

Shoulders, biceps, elbows, hair, settle
on either side / border of the frame,
suggesting a shared experience.
We have all taken our own ways
through and together returned
to this same centre.

Quiet as the students all arrive.

The old man leans down, picks
a black cast iron pot out of
the darkness behind his feet.

He shifts a cooking stand forward
from behind the fire and hangs
the pot above the flames.

He stands back.

The navy lights fade away.

The room is dark beside the fire and the glow of the moon.

The fire crackles.

END.

GALLERY HALL - INT

A large, high-ceiling room. Off-white walls, no windows. Shiny laminate birch flooring. Dark navy-blue light emits from the corners of the room, with a red-orange light flickering at the back. Hushed breathing is heard and a group of people, university students, walk on camera. A crackle is heard from the unseen fire. The ceiling is painted with silver dots. Hundreds of pieces of A4 paper hang from the ceiling on brown twine, obscuring the other side of the room, save for the shadow of something unmoving. The paper is covered in unreadable black writing.

The students are diverse in appearance and are dressed in light clothing as if it's summer; shorts, vest tops, thin hijabs, swimsuits, wrap skirts.

Beat.

Footsteps as the students enter the paper landscape as an individual page comes into focus; the writing swirls around the page as if being drawn towards the middle where it is met by an illustration of sticks arranged in a rough triangle shape.

Shadows of the students pass at the edge of the frame.

Another page comes into focus; handwritten, laid out like a letter. It ends abruptly mid-sentence.

Two students are reading another page; this one has two different types of handwriting, one clearly an imitation of the other. The writing is laid out like a conversation written down. One of the students leaves to the left.

Beat.

The other student leaves. Beat.

A crackle is heard off-screen, and the red-orange light at the back of the room flares momentarily.

More pages pass, moving closer to the red-orange light. There are fewer pages around and a wall can be seen, painted on which is a semi-realistic scene; cliffs, a night sky, faint yellow moon, ocean at the bottom.

Another crackle from an off-screen fire. Another paper comes into focus; it's this script.

Beat.

An elderly man coughs off-screen.

A hand gently pushes the paper out of the way to reveal a small fire surrounded by a ring of seashore stones. An elderly man dressed in dark colours and an unkempt beard is stood next to it. A fishing rod is stuck in the sand beside him with the line flung into an unseen corner. The fire makes him look like nothing more than a silhouette, outlining his woollen beanie and winter jacket. He stands facing the fishing line, looking out towards the painted horizon.

Shoulders and arms come into the side of the frame, facing towards the man. Hushed breathing again, footsteps come to a stop.

The man leans down, slowly picks up a previously unseen black cast iron pot and hangs it above the flame.

The navy lights fade, leaving the room in darkness save the fire and subtle glow of the painted moon.

The fire crackles.

END.

CYCLICAL

I can, I know what I mean, even if you don't. Can you see it? When do I stop this? I'm searching for it. I have a worm the way it communicate to down I cannot Maybe it's nothing. it across: going over and over whatever it was. Just a shadow with a pot of the way, just a guy. There's something here. Firelight sparkling... night - light...

There, roundabout, night-light vision ruined
Lines I'm going to write a poem about someday.
Someday soon.
Firelight sparking darkest truest red I've ever seen.
There's something here.
It is going to stick with me.
What is it? He was just a guy. Just a shadow with a pot of
fire so why do I care?
Circling it. Circling this.
Going over and over whatever it was.
Maybe it's visuals
I have a worry that, unable to draw, I cannot get it across.
Maybe it's nothing.
I'm searching for it. The way to communicate what I saw
Does that make sense? Does this?
When do I stop this?
Can you see it?   Can you see him?
I can, I know what I mean, even if you don't
Maybe that's enough.
I like the process

WRITING EXERCISE

WRITE 5 WORDS TO DESCRIBE HIM.

Bearded (maybe?)   Intimidating

Unbothered   Mysterious

          Lonely

PICTURE THE SCENE. LIST THE 3

MOST DOMINANT SENSES IN PLAY.

The touch-feel of sand worming through my socks, the chill of the air on my neck, the leftover summer-spring warmth wrapped around me.

The sound of the water, an audible boundary of where to walk and where you'd sink, the hoots and cheers and chatter of the group trailing down the angled path to the beach itself, the softer crackle of his fire.

The smell of smoke, sweet and bitter, the salt layer of the pure coastal water, the chemical makeup of a world blooming now the light had set.

WRITE A SIMILIE FOR USE IN THIS SCENE.

The night was like a living beast, kind yet tipped with sharp claws.

WRITE A METAPHOR FOR USE IN THIS SCENE.

How can one surmise a time, a place, a moment, so basic in make-up and so mechanic in emotion as this one beyond saying that the evening was but a memory played out in practice before it has been made, it was a riptide following a channel carved by itself eons ago, new yet its own history.

PLOT THE NARRATIVE OF THE STORY.

Beginning: Asking questions

Middle: Using fingernails as a screwdriver

End: ?.?.?.?

Write 5 words to describe him.

Bearded (maybe?)
Mysterious
Intimidating
Unbothered
Lonely

You Answer Here -

Picture the scene. List the three most dominant senses in play.

The touch-feel of sand worming through my socks, the chill of the air on my neck, the leftover summer-spring warmth wrapped around me.
The sound of the water, an audible boundary of where to walk and where you'd sink, the hoots and cheers and chatter of the group trailing down the angled path to the beach itself, the softer crackle of his fire.
The smell of smoke, sweet and bitter, the salt layer of the pure coastal water, the chemical makeup of a world blooming now the light had set.

You Answer Here -

Write a simile for use in this scene.

The night was like a living beast, kind yet tipped with sharp claws.

You Answer Here -

Write a metaphor for use in this scene.

How can one surmise a time, a place, a moment, so basic in make-up and so mechanic in emotion as this one beyond saying that the evening was but a memory played out in practice before it has been made, it was a riptide following a channel carved by itself eons ago, new yet its own history.

You Answer Here -

Plot the narrative of the story.

Beginning: Asking questions
Middle: Using fingernails as a screwdriver
End: ????

You Answer Here -

PLAYING WITH COLOUR

wait

wait for

a sign wait

for a hint wait

for instructions so you are sure that

the words the acts the

answer you are about

to give will be correct

wait for headlights to pass

then lead them into shadow

lead them to his heaven but

make sure you are sure there

is no room for mistake once

pen is on paper there is no

going back confuse them with the

lengths you go to to hide to be

like them crack open parts of

your mind and show them the

networks that allow you to

process then butcher your working

to see what they see do what

they do but don't let them know

how much you obsess over the process.

Wait

A sign wait

                    Wait for

                    For a hint wait

For instruction so

                    You are sure that

The words the acts the

                    Answer you are about

To give will be correct

                    Wait for headlights to pass

Then lead them into shadow

                    Lead them to his beacon but

Make sure you are sure there

                    Is no room for mistake once

Pen is on paper there is no

                    Going back confuse them
                        with the

Lengths you go to to hide to
be

                    Like them crack open parts of

Your mind and show them
the

                    Networks that allow you to

Process then butcher your
working

                    To see what they see do what

They do but don't let them
know

                    How much you obsess over
                        the process

~~took stood for phone tag dupp set to~~ the
~~following paper stood their into us excess~~
~~sit at the night silk, stood the seen~~
and a phone screen for light.

~~I am my friends of pup country eighth~~
~~hours,~~ trusted by necessity to not
harm her in her sleep.

the ~~eyes stayed against the dark,~~
~~stead listed store~~ the visual
paintings in her memory of the
road from earlier that day when
she.

~~there are~~ the marshmallows for
everyone, more than enough.

~~split~~ between the hanging left
hand of their leader of leaders and
your leader following you over
how to.

... the ... the ... as ... and sticks for roasting to others for now.

... ... of a man who didn't seem to know as she knew.

She asked for photographs to be taken of her stood in the waves, stood in the silt, stood in the – foolhardy, she tried to read the plastic-y paper of the instructions in the night with only the moon and a phone screen for light.

It was for nought and instead she – some friends of fourty-eight hours, trusted by necessity to not harm her in her sleep.

Her eyes strained against the dark, she trusted more the visual paintings in her memory of the road from earlier that day when she – he was a perfect silhouette, standing there. There were no – enough marshmallows for everyone, more than enough.

A split between the hanging left hand of their leader of leaders and your leader following you over how to – life. Stars were in the sky, a fishing line was in the air and in the sea and in the land, a tryst of the elements, a symbol of commingling, a – from the larger group to the smaller, leaving the delegation and compromises of spaces round the fire and sticks for roasting to others for now.

She knew at the time that this was something she wanted to return to but she didn't know quite – he moved the pot onto the stand above his flames and she watched, captivated, at the actions of a man who didn't seem to know as she knew.

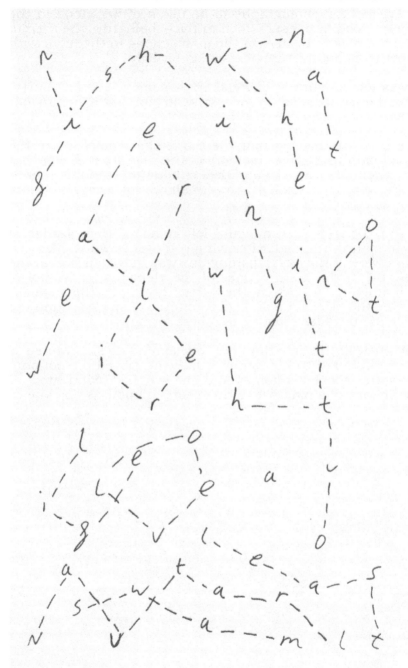

4d. e   9e. t   8b. t

5d. h   6g. l

4c. v

6d. u

9b. e

6f. a   11a. W   3a. A   9c. a

2a. I   5e. o   5f. u

10a. N

1e. i   5b. i   4a. C   7b. i   14c. r

1f. n

10c. t

6e. r   6a. N   1g. g   10b. o   12a. W

7a. L   6b. a

13a. S   7d. e

1a. F   8a. A   13c. a   11b. h

11c. e   1c. s   9d. s

5g. t

6c. t

5c. t   14d. l   14g. r   11d. n   4b. o

13d. m   9a. L   14a. E   13b. w

5a. W

1d. h   2b. n   1b. i

7c. f   14e. i   14b. a   12b. e   14f. e

1. _ _ _ _ _ _ _

2. _ _

3. _

4. _ _ _ _

5. _ _ _ _ _ _ _

6. _ _ _ _ _ _ _

7. _ _ _ _

8. _ _

9. _ _ _ _ _

10. _ _ _

11. _ _ _ _

12. _ _

13. _ _ _ _

14. _ _ _ _ _ _ _

Fill in the blanks

IS THIS POETRY?

Comprehension questions. Refer to the text ('Is This Poetry'). Write down or remember each answer in one paragraph/ page. [20 Marks]

What does the sky sound like?
Is it dark?
How is the water described?
What is the colour of the stone?
Who is there? Are they Friend or Foe? Defend Your Answer.
What is the weather like? Is it cold? Is it warm? Is it?
Where is the light coming from? What does it smell like?
Is it remembered in the same level of detail? Why? Why not?
What does each part feel like?
What are you remembering?
What are you feeling?
Are these things connected?
Nothing? What's that like? Is it calm? Is it quiet? Is it terrifying?
What are they? What is it? Does it matter?

Look at the language you have assembled together. Visual or audible, letters or signs, memories or scents, quotations or punctuation. You have written a poem. Or you have not

PACKING UP

To you, dear reader, if you so exist,
and if you so care to be known
as one who peruses words structured
in syntax so as to be legible
and understandable to those who
are familiar with the English
language.

I, to your likely knowledge by
now, have made much out of
what is in fact a memory that
grows blurrier and blurrier the
longer since the original event,
back in a spring evening after
I had risked my life descending
and ascending from sheer cliff
top to choppy waves crashing
against the rocks. I risked it
and I swam best I could and
I set my boundaries, I said
yes and I said no. I ruled

the world with adrenaline in
my blood, bouncing, electrifying,
draining each and every tiny
cell in my veins, my capillaries,
my arteries.

This is to say, I have made
much out of a moment that
lasted at most two hours
and at least a second.

I have used it in ways I hope
have made no sense whatsoever
to you. I have used it in an
attempt to teach you something.
I have used it to show you
some of me and to reflect parts
of you.

Perhaps you have found things here, picked them up, held them to the light to see the smoothed down sea glass edges, ran your thumbs across the scalloped ridges, tested the weight in palms. I give you permission to pocket them. I will also watch if you ship them away, counting the jumps, one, two, three.

I'm nearly done with this now. Soon it will be yours, soon you will exist. A self-fulfilling prophecy, in a way. Thank you, reader, for reading. I gift this to you. I will give you no answers, no hints, no walkthroughs, no toolkits through which to pick apart and understand, no.

No.

This is yours to do, yours to puzzle out. Or yours to leave behind. Yours to linger over. Yours to forget entirely. Enjoy, whichever you decide.

To you, dear reader, if you so exist, and if you so care to be known as one who peruses words structured in syntax so as to be legible and understandable to those who are familiar with the English language.

I, to your likely knowledge by now, have made much out of what is in fact a memory that grows blurrier and blurrier the longer since the original event, back in a spring evening after I had risked my life descending and ascending from sheer cliff top to choppy waves crashing against the rocks. I risked it and I swam best I could and I set my boundaries, I said yes and I said no. I ruled the world with adrenaline in my blood, bouncing, electrifying, draining each and every tiny cell in my veins, my capillaries, my arteries.

This is to say, I have made much out of a moment that lasted at most two hours and at least a second.

I have used it in ways I hope have made no sense whatsoever to you. I have used it in an attempt to teach you something. I have used it to show you some of me and to reflect parts of you.

Perhaps you have found things here, picked them up, held them to the light to see the smoothed down sea glass edges, ran your thumb across the scalloped ridges, tested the weight in palms. I give you permission to pocket them. I will also watch if you skip them away, counting the jumps, one, two, three.

I'm nearly done with this now. Soon it will be yours, soon you will exist. A self-fulfilling prophecy, in a way. Thank you, reader, for reading. I gift this to you. I will give you no answers, no hints, no walkthroughs, no tool kits through which to pick apart and understand, no. No.

This is yours to do, yours to puzzle out. Or yours to leave behind. Yours to linger over. Yours to forget entirely. Enjoy, whichever you decide.

ACKNOWLEDGEMENTS

Hey! Welcome! Good to see you, I too enjoy reading the acknowledgements of a book so let's get started. This is going to be a lot of thanks and some fun references you won't get but can infer things about my life from. A real exercise in investigating a person!

Thank you, first of all, to my Mum. Hi Mama! Hope work was all good! Thank you for supporting me when I didn't know I needed support, thank you for being my rock, my foundation, my fountain of knowledge, and my calm in the storm. Thank you for trying over and over and over and learning and listening. Thank you. I love you loads and loads. You are my favourite person in the whole world, forever and always.

Thank you to my brothers whom I cannot name individually because privacy but also because then there's a hierarchy and I can't be doing with that debate. I love you both so, so much. Hope the glasses are good, youngest one! You should really have them by now but as I'm writing this you haven't yet so here we are. Thank you for always trusting me, for listening to me, but most especially for talking to me, thank you for sharing your life and hobbies and stories with me. Thank you, middlest one, for your unwavering support, for calling me to walk me home in the dark, for making me laugh, for making me cups of tea, for being you. I'm so unbelievably proud of you. Of both of you. I adore you both.

Thank you to my dad and all my grandparents for all your love and support. I love you all.

Thank you to the rest of my family, you haven't been left out, no jokes about leaving you out please and thank you!

Thank you to Becca, my wonderful publisher who took a punt on a girl who wrote a short story in about two days and still was under word count and who then still wanted to work with me to publish this collection. Thank you so much. You are amazing, never forget that.

Thank you to Ada. You may not realise it but you inspired a lot of the start of this collection. It wouldn't be what it is without you. Thank you for working with us and thank you for making what I know will be an incredible space (you haven't finished making it yet, I just have absolute faith in you).

Thank you to CJ and Jo for making our years living together in Wales the best years of my life, through a pandemic and through every karaoke night and hyper-fixation. I wouldn't be who I am today without you both. All my love. Thank you to the Gays (you know who you are but also all the queer people reading this, you can count yourselves too if you wish) for making me laugh and continuing to welcome me back to Wales.

Thank you to Adnan and Hayley. For listening. For loving me and recognising the ways I love you. Thank you to Caitlin, my longest, oldest friend. Thank you for sticking by me since we were like four years old, the one I always think of first when someone asks if anyone can read my writing.

Thank you to Undeb Bangor, especially Katie and Rhiannon, for an amazing trip that I clearly have extremely fond memories of. Thank you to Joey and my Experimental Writing module classmates for encouraging me with my poetry and for taking the time to decode my handwriting.

Thank you to our wonderful illustrator!!

Finally, a slightly more amorphous one, thank you to my friends, my acquaintances, my co-workers. Thank you to those online, those I follow on social media, those who post YouTube videos that have me relaxing for the first time all day, those who make the music I listen to as I write and eat and walk and live, and especially to those who have read and commented and bookmarked my AO3 stories since I was fifteen. Thank you for being my teachers, my friends, my editors, my companions, my jesters, my people, my terrible idiots.

The Fisherman is more than just a book - you can now interact with the book in a new way. Created by Ada Null, this gallery displays the original handwritten notes that made the book what it is today.

www.barnardpublishing.co.uk/the-fisherman-gallery

Printed in Great Britain
by Amazon

20083368R00059